How To Be The Almost
Perfect Wife

By Husbands Who Know

How To Be The Almost
Perfect Wife

By Husbands Who Know

COMPILED BY J. S. SALT

To all my contributors

∾

Copyright © 2000 by J.S. Salt

Published by
Shake It! Books
P.O. Box 6565
Thousand Oaks, CA 91359
Toll Free: (877) Shake It
www.**shake**that**brain**.com

This book is available at special discounts for bulk purchase for sales promotions, premiums, fund-raising and educational use.
Special books, or book excerpts, can also be created to fit specific needs.

ISBN: 0-9667156-2-4
10 9 8 7 6 5 4 3 2 1
First Edition

These are my principles.
If you don't like them, I have others.

—GROUCHO MARX

Contents

Introduction

Why don't husbands like to open up and share their feelings?

Because they're men.

This book, in fact, took two years of begging nearly one thousand men. *Talk with me, please. Let me know what you need from your wives.* Which is why this book came to be—so wives could learn what their husbands crave; and husbands, at the very least, could point and say: *See, that's what I need. Just like this guy says on page _____.*

Guaranteed. The book you now hold in your hands will serve as *a catalyst for conversation,* leading you and your spouse to better understanding ... and a better marriage.

Or give this insider's guide, and its companion volume, *How to Be the Almost Perfect Husband—By Wives Who Know,* to a couple that's *about* to get married.

These small but important books will surely improve any union or marriage. They've even improved my own marriage. (And it was pretty good *before* the books.)

J.S. Salt

Support

Believe in me,
believe in me,
believe in me.

— ALAN, 29
married 1 day

Be my cheerleader. Believe that I have the talent to achieve my dreams, even if it takes longer than I ever imagined.

— ED, 47
married 25 years

Help me be a hero to my kids. Speak well of me and the good things that I do. Don't only speak about my shortcomings.

— NORMAN, 67
divorced after 22 years

Just as I tell our kids,
"I love you and I'm proud of you,"
I need to hear the same from you:
That you love me and you're proud of me
as a husband and a dad.

— ALEX, 37
married 12 years

When you tell me you're proud of me
it gives me a boost—especially when
I'm beating myself up, mad at myself
for not being Bill Gates.

— JOEL, 47
married 5 years

A husband needs constant words of admiration and respect. He can get some of that at work and from others, but he craves it most from his wife.

— DAVE, 39
married 1 day

Respect your husband. Despite all his faults (which you know better than anyone else), let him know often that you think he is great and that you admire him.

— DAVID, 49
married 26 years

Copy my wife. She has put up with my crotchety ways for 50 years and acted like she enjoyed it. She doesn't always agree with me or care for some of the things I do, but she makes it clear that she *always* loves me. And that's pretty good.

— PATRICK, 71
married 50 years

Be my advocate, be on my side.
If you think I'm wrong, try to guide me
to where you think I should be.
Don't beat me up and drag me there.

— CHARLIE, 28
married 11 years

Empower your husband to make
the best choice or decision, then walk
away from the situation. To constantly
repeat is perceived as *nagging*.

— RHONNE, 46
married 12 years

Keep telling me when I screw up,
but do it quietly, matter-of-factly, lovingly,
and when we're alone.

— BILL, 69
2nd marriage of 23 years

Know when to push
and when to ease off.

— ANDY, 37
married 3 years

When I am self critical
is not the time
to heap it on.

— RICK, 55
married 20 years

When I'm telling a story don't interrupt me by correcting every little detail. The facts aren't what's important. What is important is supporting me and making me look good—not like some fool who can't get his facts straight!

— MIKE, 48
2nd marriage of 6 years

Listen to my stories, even if you find them boring. They're not boring to me so I must be telling them to you for a reason.

— MICHAEL, 27
married 5 years

Listen attentively to your husband's dreams and aspirations. Even if you think they're unreachable, humor him. Support him. Maybe even get excited with him. Your husband will love and appreciate you because you encouraged—rather than discouraged—him. Later in life, a husband wants to look at his wife and say, "Honey, you were *with* me," Not "If only..."

— ROLLAND, 64
married 42 years

Understand that dreaming is the blueprint for
reality. Nurture your partner's dreams.
Give him the support he needs to become
the person he wants to be.

— EDDY, 51
2nd marriage of 26 years

Be a friend who is there to lend support,
but still cares enough to confront me
when I make a fool of myself.

— TERRY, 53
2nd marriage of 23 years

We don't like to ask for directions
when we're lost.
We don't like to ask for directions
when we're "lost" in life.
When you see I'm lost, find a way
to gently guide me back.

— KEVIN, 39
married 12 years

Be patient with us:
We're men.
Make us feel special:
We're boys.

— TOBY, 33

Men are just boys who need attention and reassurance — pretty much all the time. They need you to sit on their laps, kiss them for no reason and assure them that you love them.

— JIM, 80
married 23 and 30 years, widower

Acceptance

Accept your husband as the man he is,
instead of wishing you could change
things here and there.

— CHARLES, 38

Saying, "Jane's husband always helps
with the shopping, why can't you?"
makes me want to say,
"Why didn't you marry Jane's husband?"

— ALLEN, 43
married 2 years

Accept that I'm not "escaping" to work:
I'm going there because I *need* to work.
Besides, when I feel better about my work,
I feel better about everything else.

— ERIC

It's a fact: Every husband needs at least 2 hours a week on the couch in front of the TV— without having to answer any questions. Just to veg out.

— RAY, 39
married 7 years

Respect the power of Monday Night Football.

— ALAN, 29
married 1 day

Respect my right to sit back with a beer
and enjoy the game in peace.
The garbage can wait, questions can wait,
and so can just about anything else.

— TOM, 45
married 3 years

Stop trying to control and change us so much.
We're not "diamonds in the rough"—we're men.
The same men you fell in love with
and married in the first place.

— BILL, 47
2nd marriage of 6 months

Thanks for letting me be myself, not trying
to change me into some "ideal" you wanted
most of all—just as I have not tried to change you,
but accept you for what and who you are.

—ALAN, 74
married 55 years

Every now and then, let me enjoy
a cigar. I'd enjoy it even more
without your sly disapproval.

— Izzy, 42
married 12 years to "a 99% approving wife"

> A good cigar is as great a comfort to a
> man as a good cry is to a woman.
>
> —E.G. BULWER-LYTTON

Trust my judgement without
questioning everything
– especially on the small stuff.

– JOHN, 27
married 7 years

Limit your criticisms to things that really matter. (And when you get impatient with your husband, don't grit your teeth but remember your love for him and truly feel it.)

— BEN, 81
"happily married for 55 years,
despite some humongous ups and downs"

Treat your husband with the
same degree of respect you have
for your mom and dad.

— BILL, 57
2nd marriage of 16 years

Treat my children from my previous marriage as if they were your own.

— PAUL, 38
2nd marriage, "6 years and wobbly"

Stop criticizing my mother.
I know she's not perfect and
I have my own issues with her.
But I don't need added pressure from you.

— ALFRED, 68
3rd marriage of 13 years

Accept my parents as I accept yours.
When they're around, I need you
to be cordial and friendly—
if not for them, for the man you love.

— RON, 40
married 6 years

Be tolerant of your in-laws.

— GENE, 76
married 56 years

If you get mad at me, I don't expect you to get over it the next minute. Just keep in mind that not everything is a *hanging crime*. So try to show some mercy and forgive me when you can.

— ROBERT, 41
2nd marriage of 1 year

Always have patience when mine runs out.

— ALLEN, 33
married 1 year

Accept my weaknesses
but help me to improve.

— DEREK, 45
divorced twice, about to be married again

I know how difficult I can be sometimes.
(Lots of times.) Just try to understand
I'm *trying* to do good,
no matter how bad I may sometimes act.

— LEN

Don't dwell on my mistakes all the time.
Remember the good as well as the bad.

— MATT, 28
married 6 years

All men make mistakes, but married
men find out about them sooner.

— RED SKELTON

As the two of you work to build your marriage,
your husband will make mistakes: He will
bend a lot of nails, miswire the bathroom fan,
put up a wall in the wrong place,
even build an entire room you didn't want.
When he finishes, celebrate.
Don't focus on all his mistakes:
Keep the big picture in mind.

— DAN, 54
divorced after 24 years

Let your man do all the repair work
and remodeling he wants.
And don't belittle him if it's not perfect.
Admire what he has done.

— HOWIE, 78
3rd marriage of 11 years

The one thing I wanted most from
my two wives was appreciation.
If only they had shown me
they were glad I was their husband.

— JIM, 80
married 23 and 30 years, widower

Communication

Two words of advice
for a long term marriage:

"Yes, dear."

And that goes for both of you!

— JOHN, 71
married 48 years

Be willing to admit your mistakes
and say "I'm sorry" when appropriate.
It's not *always* the man's fault.

— MIKE, 44
divorced after 3 years

Admit when you're wrong
and I'll try to do the same for you.

— RUDY, 47
2nd marriage of 5 years

> Whenever you're wrong, admit it;
> Whenever you're right, shut up.
>
> —OGDEN NASH

When you're upset about something,
talk to me about it. Don't let it become
a landmine that later explodes.

— NORMAN, 32
married 5 years

If I ask you what's wrong, *tell* me.
Don't say "Nothing" and then expect me
to guess what it is.

— KEVIN, 42
married 19 years

Listen to how your husband feels,
even if you have to drag it out of him.
Letting emotions bottle up can lead
to a big mess over time.

— ALBERTO, 34
divorced

I love it when you just listen to show you understand. I also love it when you challenge me with a different perspective.

— JEFF, 43
married 17 years

Please don't assume that everything I say
has been carefully thought out before I say it.
So don't "hang me" because
I choose a wrong word, or say something
in a way that raises your hackles.

— ALLEN, 43
married 2 years

Stop trying to finish all my sentences for me.
Remember: I'm a man with a boy's ego
and must, just must, have my say.

— JAY, 62
married 30 years

When I make a suggestion
and you turn it down, that's one thing.
But when someone else says the same
thing and you go, "What a great idea!"
it makes me feel like you take my ideas
—*and me!*—for granted.

— STEWART, 37
married 7 years

Try to learn the difference between
Hearing and Understanding.
Sometimes I know you "hear" me but
I wonder if you "understand" me.

— DAN, 75
married 53 years

First, try to understand.
Then, try to be understood.

— CHARLES, 34
married 6 years

The first duty of love is to listen.

— PAUL TILLICH

When all I get is complaints and negative feedback from you, it makes me feel like I must be the worst husband in the world. Spend some time telling me about the *good* you see. Tell me how I'm doing with the kids, how I make you happy (if I do), how I make your life easier (if I do) and what you think is *good* about me. Bottom line: Don't just tell me what's wrong with me, tell me what's *right*, as well.

— JERRY, 53
2nd marriage of 5 years

Pay attention to your man. Compliment him.
And don't be too critical or berate him.
He probably already knows his shortcomings.

— GERARDO, 29
divorced after 1 1/2 years

The expression "I told you so"
—either verbally or with body language—
is never productive in building up your mate.

— DICK, 64
married 43 years

Don't be afraid to have arguments in front of your kids. That way, they can learn that strife and different opinions can be resolved by using good manners and having respect for each other. Then your children will say, "Okay. We can have arguments—but we watched Mom and Dad resolve it the right way!"

— NIC, 51
2nd marriage of 24 years

Remember that many things
we discuss are confidential and
should not be repeated to anyone else.

— DICK, 64
married 45 years

Don't tell my friends bad things
about me.

— LEE, 61
divorced

Please, let's not talk about bills or finances
right before we go to sleep
—because then I *can't* go right to sleep.

— JOEL, 47
married 5 years

Originally the plan was, no discussion of unpleasantries while getting ready for bed ... but there's something about putting a toothbrush in your mouth that makes people want to talk.

— PAUL REISER

Only start a conversation
if I'm in the room with you.

— CHARLES, 34
married 6 years

Please listen and remember, so I don't have to
keep repeating myself. It makes me think
you don't listen to me anymore. And
please stop saying, "That never happened."

— JOHN, 72
2nd marriage of 20 years

Have the patience to learn to truly communicate.
(Being a person with a profound hearing
impairment, it took me *tons of patience.*)
Being able to communicate with your heart
and mind is the key to unlock most any door.

— JAMES, 45
married 13 years

Differences

I don't know who said: "Never go to bed angry at each other" but I suspect that person wasn't married. Just remember: If we go to bed angry now and then, it doesn't mean we're headed for divorce.

— ROBERT, 43
married 7 years

You have to fight. If you don't, you are not in a healthy relationship. So we have a few arguments to clear the air, like most couples.

— LIAM NEESON

If I want to go to bed later than you
it doesn't mean I don't love you. It means
I want to go to bed later than you.

— NEAL, 47
married 12 years

I wish you wouldn't insist that we do what you
want precisely at the moment you want to do it.
At least find out if it's a good time for me.

— ROLAND, 41
married 5 years

Understand that your time frame and
your husband's may not be the same.
Just because *you* say it's time to do something,
don't expect your husband to jump right in line.

— TOBY, 33

Be willing to compromise,
then join forces.
Marriage is like a row boat.
If both partners row together
they will surely make progress.

— BRADLEY, 54
married 26 years

Accept that there are things I like to do
that are typical "men things."
When you see me doing these things
—and enjoying myself—don't look at me
as though I'm a retro-minded Neanderthal.

— SCOTT, 44
married 15 years

When I go out to play sports or be with the guys,
I'm not taking something away
—you're giving *me* something I need.
Women want flowers? Guys want to
have time with each other without having
to justify themselves for being away a few hours.

— ERIC, 28
married 6 years

Encourage him to develop interests
outside the relationship:
Two halves don't make a whole.
Only two wholes make a whole.

— LARRY, 46
2nd marriage of 18 years

Independent social lives are essential
to a long standing relationship.
Monday Night Football with the guys
comes to mind.

— STEPHEN, 30
married 8 years

Give me more space without obsessing
about why I'd rather be alone than
with you at that particular moment.

— MITCHELL, 50
married 6 years

When I ask for space it doesn't mean
I don't love you or that I'm abandoning you:
I just need time to regroup.

— GARY, 41
married 12 years

Silence can be a good thing.
Just because I'm not talking or
"sharing" all the time doesn't mean
there's a problem.

— DON, 51
married 30 years

If I have a problem,
let me go off and sulk for a while.
That's my way of coping.

— COLIN

A room of one's own—if only for
a few hours a day—is the most
important room in the house.
A smart wife knows that if her husband
feels like reading or watching TV
and she wants to go to a movie
—to separate is sublime!

— LEO, 67
married 48 years

When you need to be alone,
don't expect me to read your mind.
Just ask for your space and you'll get it.
After all, if there's one thing guys
understand—it's the need for space.

— DENNIS, 48
married 16 years

If I mention an old girlfriend,
try not to be jealous.
I married you, not her.

— ROBERT, 43
married 7 years

Don't tell me stories about your ex-lovers.
I know you married me
but it still makes me jealous.

— MITCHELL, 50
married 6 years

Never donate old favorite things of his to charity without his permission. A wife who forgot this rule donated an old pair of boots to a school rummage sale. She discovered (too late) that the boots contained several thousand dollars in "walking around money."

— JOHN, 55
2nd marriage of 20 years

Stop asking me to throw out
my torn, faded, "looks-like-you-lived-in
them-for-a-hundred-years" jeans.
What you hate about them is
exactly what I love about them.

— ANDY, 45
married 11 years

Decide quickly what to order from a menu.
When you take forever to decide,
most men silently go out of their minds.

— JOHN, 55
2nd marriage of 20 years

Sex & Adventure

I love it when you touch me unexpectedly, when you run your hand along my neck and whisper sweet nothings in my ear.

— STEVE, 58
married 15 years

I love it when you seduce me—when you act sexy and talk dirty to me—and when you leave nail marks on my back.

— ROLAND, 41
married 5 years

Dress sexy for me.
And not just before bed.

— MITCHELL, 47
married 12 years

More than once a year, wear
that lacy nightie I bought you.

— KIRK, 37
married 12 years

Ask me:
"What are your sexual fantasies
and how can I get you there?"

— MICHAEL, 49
married 12 years

> Husbands are like fires.
> They go out if unattended.
>
> — ZSA ZSA GABOR

I need you to take the lead sometimes
—in daily life and in bed. Sometimes I want
you to navigate so I can just enjoy the ride.

— FRED, 53
married 19 years

Pounce on me unexpectedly.

— LAURENCE, 33
married 4 years

Let's set aside the time
*—and energy—*for plenty of
fun, creative, exciting, energizing sex.

— MASON, 43
2nd marriage of 12 years

It would be nice to have a romantic
sojourn with you where we could recapture
some of the early bliss we shared.
It's all too dry a life;
we must get the romance back.

— JAY, 62
married 30 years

Be more spontaneous.
If I say, *Let's go have an adventure,*
don't worry about fixing your hair
or making reservations.
Nothing kills my spontaneity more.

— NORMAN, 74
married 48 years

After your picture-perfect party,
laugh, and let me muss your hair.

— DUKE, 63
married 42 years

I love your fancy cooking,
but it's keeping us from
making love more often.

— JAMES, 56
married 38 years

Every night let me know if you:
a) want to cuddle
b) want passionate sex
c) want to be left the heck alone.

— JEFF, 36
married 5 years

After we have sex, try not to say,
"Why don't we do this more often?"
It tends to take a great feeling and
make me feel inadequate somehow.

— LARRY, 36
married 5 years

Passion is everything!
I need you to be passionate and
want me physically as I want you.

— DEREK, 45
divorced twice, about to be married again

Friendship. Friendship carries a couple through more hard times than passion.

— THOMAS, 55
married 29 years

Day to Day

Try not to put my needs last all the time:
the kids, the dogs, your parents.
I feel like I get you (and your attention)
only when everyone *else* has
been taken care of.

— GORDON, 39
married 12 years

When you give the kids vitamins,
remember to give me one as well.

— DAVID, 38
married 16 years

When you go to the store,
ask me, "Is there something
special I can get for you?"

— BLAIR, 53
2nd marriage of 7 years

1. Think about my needs
before your own.
2. Learn that a home-cooked meal
is an act of love.
3. Do both these things and I will
do the same for you.

— CARY, 44
married 11 years

Instead of saying, "The man does this, the woman does that," let's see which of us likes or does something best and let that determine how we divide up our responsibilities.

— BILL, 65
married 43 years

Every once in a while, surprise me by taking out the garbage. I've been taking out the garbage since I was a kid.

— ETHAN, 32
married 3 years

Trade off with each other on doing
the bills. That way you both know
what your life is really costing.

— JOHN, 55
2nd marriage of 20+ years

Do not volunteer your husband's efforts without having an initial consultation with him. After all, it's his time and effort you're volunteering.

— DAVID, 37
married 5 years

Don't over commit us with lots of
social activities and things we "have to do."
What we "have to do" is focus first on us.

— JOEL, 47
married 5 years

Look good for me and for yourself.

— GERARDO, 29
divorced after 1½ years

On the days (or years) he's not looking like such a bargain, remember when he was brand new and still had hair. Then remember when you used to laugh at his bad jokes and kiss his pot belly. Finally, say to yourself, as many times as needed, until it sinks in: "I'm not perfect either. I'm not perfect either. I'm not perfect either."

— FRANK, 48
married 16 years

Every moment should be treasured
when we're together.
Don't let "life" get in the way.
Our relationship is a special gift that
deserves nothing less than Top Priority.

— STAN, 45
married 7 years

a. Worry less.
b. Be goofier.

— MITCHELL, 50
married 6 years

Keep making countless decisions without me that make our lives and our children's lives better.

— JEFF, 43
married 17 years

Continue to help our children learn through love and encouragement.

— RON, 44

Keep yourself connected to your friends
and life goals so you remain vital and new.

— TERRY, 53
2nd marriage of 23 years

Never let me take you for granted.

— ALLEN, 33
married 1 year

Never doubt that I love you
with all my heart.

— RON, 52
married 30 years

Change nothing,
stay as perfect as you are.
I only wish I could have been
as perfect for you.

— STEVE, 63
married 41 years

My Requests

(Notes to my wife)